A Perfect Day for Semaphore

poems by

Holly Day

Finishing Line Press
Georgetown, Kentucky

A Perfect Day for Semaphore

Copyright © 2018 by Holly Day
ISBN 978-1-63534-682-4 First Edition
All rights reserved under International and Pan-American Copyright Conventions.
No part of this book may be reproduced in any manner whatsoever without written permission from the publisher, except in the case of brief quotations embodied in critical articles and reviews.

ACKNOWLEDGMENTS

"Remolding" appeared in *Disturbed Digest* June 2016
"Barricade" and "Down to the Water" appeared in *Guide to Kulchur Creative Journal* #7
"The Man" appeared in *Mystery and Horror* #2
"Nebraska" appeared in *The Minaret Vol. 65* #19
"A New Vocabulary" appeared in *Teen Anthem* #1
"Some Babies Just Know" appeared in *Poets' Espresso Review* Vol. 9 #31
"Spoilsport" and "Fingers Pull a Shoulder Strap Down" appeared in *Disturbed Digest* June 2016
"Overnight" appeared in *Mystery and Horror* #2
"slowly" appeared in *Big Scream 43*
"Afternoons with My Stepmother" appeared in *Whistling Shade* Vol. 13 #2
"The Ferret" appeared in *Yomimono* #7
"That Day" *Lilliput Review* #193
"Hands Fold Like Dying Butterflies" appeared in *fourW* #25
"Lection" appeared in *Neon Literary Magazine* #38

Publisher: Leah Maines

Editor: Christen Kincaid

Cover Art: Sherman Wick, Durand, WI photos

Author Photo: Wolfgang Wick

Cover Design: Elizabeth Maines McCleavy

Printed in the USA on acid-free paper.
Order online: www.finishinglinepress.com

Author inquiries and mail orders:
Finishing Line Press
P. O. Box 1626
Georgetown, Kentucky 40324
U. S. A.

Table of Contents

1	Sunshine
2	Passenger A
3	Shades
4	Unchanging More Fixed
5	Loss
6	The Wings of Black Crows
7	Bad Things Happened
8	The Sacred Texts
9	Unfurling
10	The Rite of Exploration
11	At the Stop
12	The Day the Leaves Started to Change
13	Why Not
14	The Stories We Tell
15	Confession
16	Orange
17	The Cavemen
18	The Dove
19	Remolding
20	Barricade
21	Down to the Water
22	A Test of Vows and Faith
23	The Old Green One
24	Two Minutes Thirteen Seconds
25	The First of Many
26	I've Taken to Writing Suicide Notes
27	The Middle of the Night
28	Blue Car
29	Nebraska
30	A New Vocabulary
31	Some Babies Just Know
32	Spoilsport

33	Fingers Pull a Shoulder Strap Down
34	Overnight
35	The Nest
36	The Funeral
37	Sparrow Poem #1
38	The Lover of Zeus
39	Thursday, A Little Before the School Bus is Due
40	Kiss It All Away
41	For My Grandfather
42	The Offering
43	Upon the Discovery of the Existence of Another Golden Calf
44	Ghost Father Father
45	Hillsboro Bay
46	When Summer Comes
47	Extractions
48	Winter
49	Morning at the Beach
50	I didn't miss you at all when you left.
51	slowly
52	This House
53	Conversations Deferred
54	Lithogenous
55	Afternoons with My Stepmother
56	The Ferret
57	That Day
58	Hands Fold Like Dying Butterflies
59	Lection
60	Early Spring Walk

For Sherman, always.

Sunshine

She puts the pillow over his face and prays
it'll be as easy as the shows she's seen on TV.
He pulls it away, laughs and tells her he still has to go
she is no match for him tonight. The moon
lights up the fields outside, all around the house, and she
and this house are a plague ship on a dead sea
there is no reason for anyone to stay here, even if only
to ride it out until the next town.

Alone, she imagines he's kissed her goodbye, on the cheek
soft as a little girl's whisper, an echo of sunset.
When she brings him the baby, he won't ask
about the random things he's left behind at her house
the other men's shoes in her closet.
When she comes to his house
swollen with starlight,
he won't be able to slip out the door as if
she is nothing but air.

Passenger A

I reached across her mini-skirted lap
opened the car door
pushed her out. the joke's
gone too far, I said as she
stumbled to the curb.

thanks for the ride anyway, she shouted
flipping me off. and yes, I do remember you
from that place
from that thing
I just didn't want to say anything
because I didn't want you to know
I knew you back then
because I thought it might fuck you up
embarrass you
you were a real asshole back then
just like now.

a few seconds after I drove away,
I watched her flag down another car
get in and disappear. It was a better car than mine
passed me going fast down the road
carrying that bitch with it
I thought I saw her face in the window as it passed
she looked scared.
I thought about

following the car
seeing where it was taking her
if maybe she needed me to save her from something
but she was such a fucking bitch to me
back then
at that place
I figured that even now
she wasn't worth the trouble.

Shades

When her husband disappeared, it was easy
to imagine he'd been stolen. First, by another woman
someone younger, some pale sylph
with dark, wild eyes and long black hair
or perhaps an older woman far richer than she would ever be
who promised a world he had only dreamed existed—
The wife without a husband railed against
these phantom women.

Later, when no explanatory letter surfaced in the mail
no muffled apologies came by way of telephone
the phantom women grew ominous, sprouted
sharp, jagged fingernails on their long white fingers
vampire teeth and rusted switchblades.
She began to wait for ransom notes to appear
slipped into the mailbox after the regular delivery
tucked under her pillow by mysterious hands.

It was almost a relief when the police found his body
wrapped around the bridge footings
under the ice. Married friends who had avoided her
thinking she'd been abandoned
crept out of the shadows to offer condolences
bearing casseroles and foil-wrapped pies
as though they could replace the emptiness left
with comfort food, as though they sincerely believed that food
could comfort. "It's all right," she'd say to these friends
quietly through the tears, the perfect, grieving widow.
"At least now I know where he is."

Unchanging More Fixed

I am a ghost invisible I am
quiet and cold here in the dark
I am becoming nothing
I am becoming

his hand moves across me and I
grind my teeth trying not to feel
people meet my gaze as I walk down the street
it all falls inside me shrinks to nothing
falls right through me shrinks to nothing

push down the memories
ball them up and hide them in place
I am becoming nothing
nobody notices as I sit at my desk
nothing nothing nothing nothing

Loss

I look for it everywhere, the magic
I used to see around me. I carefully check
beneath cushions before I vacuum
approach dark, spiderwebbed corners with gentle hands
lie awake to the sound of the house settling
the mice scampering in the attic, holding my breath
hoping that it's there.

I watch my daughter playing in the yard
singing to earthworms and dancing with toads
and I know she sees all the magical things
I'm missing. I join in on her games
make fairy houses out of mud and broken seashells

share stories of how wonderful it would be
if we were frogs or fairies ourselves
and I can tell she believes
we could be those things if we really wanted to be
that being just what we are is some sort of choice
I can tell she believe this
and I wish I could, too.

The Wings of Black Crows

They were as powerful as they were exotic, ghosts
of terror, the flapping of stained sheets
just out of sight. Their eyes bent spades into old train cars
huddled shadows in the rusty quiet, dreams of wheels turning.

I wanted so badly to stand in the room as a light
to take a small bit of their pain into me and survive it all
next time; they will have to wait. There are more bodies
in the lake out back that need to be counted. My visions can wait.

Bad Things Happened

We could feel the spirits only when we sat by the
walls. There was something left behind by those who sat
just there, under His eyes, in the back row of hard, wooden pews
the fear of God. There was such an obvious difference between where
the good Christians and the bad Christians sat in that place.

They were as powerful as they were exotic, the ghosts
of terror, His omniscience, the flapping of stained sheets
just out of sight. Their eyes bent spades into old train cars
huddled shadows in the rusty quiet, dreams of wheels turning.

I wanted so badly to stand in the room as a light
to take a small bit of their pain into me and survive it all
next time. There are bodies in the lake out back
that need to be counted. My visions can wait
but He will never come.

The Sacred Texts

I would have had so many more poems to show you
but the priest destroyed them all when he came
said my pre-Columbian ideals, my life before him, were wrong
told me I was wrong. I stood by, penitent, as he hauled

box after box of handwritten journals
out to the curb to melt in the rain, came back
covered in sweat and ink to remind me
it was for the best, he only wanted the best

for me. I watched the codices that had recorded my life before him
disintegrate through the crack in the curtains, pretending
to keep an eye on children bicycling in the rain
that I was impatient for the mail. I watched

as history, deprived of its tongue
forgot all about me.

Unfurling

The dust finally settles, and it's safe to come out.
Doors of fallout shelters creak open,
exhale recycled air and the smell
of confinement. The first step
cautiously out into the open.

Huddled masses stretch themselves into the halls
of new palaces: abandoned, themed McDonald's
massive stock exchange buildings bearing reliefs of
extinct flowers and grains
an ice skating rink, big enough
for children and horses.

Self-proclaimed kings and queens
spontaneously create new religions
and traditions, declare them in a competition of cacophony
through broken skyscraper windows
and flimsy observation decks
littered with the bodies of sparrows and pigeons.

The Rite of Exploration

You make me want to drill holes in my skull
wrap wires around my brain, sink drill bits and fingertips into
my body, map the lace of fine blood vessels
with radioactive dyes, trace my skeleton through my skin
with melted solder and #2 pencils
dig a place inside me for you to curl up and sleep
never leave. I want you to have it all:

my skin to wrap in a sheet around your shoulders
or around your waist when you step out of the bath
my skull and pelvis to prop open the door
when you need to bring new furniture into the house
fingers and toes to shim under wobbly table legs and chairs
the rest of my blood to stain the floor more evenly
to match the spot on the wood where I fell.

At the Stop

I take the dog out to the bus stop to wait
For my daughter to come home from school. One of the other mothers
Has driven to the bus stop, and she sits in her car with the windows rolled up
Maybe she's listening to music, or just enjoying the quiet.

The dog starts digging at something and I push at her with my foot
Make her stop, this isn't her yard. She sits down and wags her tail
Pushes against my leg for comfort. I pet her large, blocky head
Tell her the bus is coming soon.

I look up and see the woman in the car
Is watching me, I think. She's wearing mirrored sunglasses
And I can't tell if she's watching me or just fallen asleep
Her head pressed against the window, jaw slightly open as though
Something I'm doing is really interesting, or maybe
She's just slipped into a coma or she's dead.

The school bus pulls up and I wait to see if the woman moves
If I have to carefully walk her daughter to the car to see what's wrong
If I have to brace her little girl with the horrible news that her mother
Has just died, right there, sitting in the car while waiting for her to come home.
And how wonderful would that be, I think, as I see the woman straighten up
Unlock the doors of her car with a noisy "click," to say

You were such a devoted mother that even though you knew
Deep in your heart that something was physically wrong, that you
Should probably go to the doctor instead of the bus stop, that even so
You still drove your car the two blocks to the bus stop to wait
For the bus to pull up and end your day.

The Day the Leaves Started to Change

The bird flutters into the church like some sort of portent
disturbs the service with a flurry of feathers. It would be nice
if it was a dove, or some brilliant, golden, phoenix-type of bird
but it's just a sparrow come in from the cold.

The preacher waits until the bird has settled before continuing on
with his speech, but he is distracted. Every time the bird
moves to another corner of the church, he instinctively covers the top
of his bald head with one robed arm as if
too used to having birds shit on him

while flying overhead.

Why Not

He tells me, I swear if you stay on the drugs
I will never leave. He puts them in my hand
I make a fist around the little pills
that will keep him here
careful not to drop them.

I fill my head with songs I learned
in school long ago, memories
of the men who came before him
that didn't mind my little rainbows
never made me beg for sweetness.

The Stories We Tell

I feel the wings flutter under my skin as I tell them
about my childhood, about how things were before
I had children of my own. I hint at the type of insect I was
make it more beautiful—I was a butterfly, a damselfly
a fluorescent leaf-hopper, something amazing.

Because they're my children, I can tell they believe me
that right now, they're imagining me as
a lime-green lunar moth, wing soft as down
not the chitinous beetle I really was
brown and dull and unimportant,
scuttling from one crack to the next.

Confession

The bird hides inside, tucked inside my ribcage
too rotten to present. Bodies twist, limbs flail
but I didn't come.

Dark and black and wet, he's swimming
in the sweat of other women, rotten
to the heart. The bird is in here, barely visible
in the sick hot summer, intent on

murdering angels.
Even through the cigarette smoke and birthday cologne
he's in my heart—I can smell him.

Orange

To fight the subtle constant helplessness
I have begun painting my skeleton
color-coding the days as each piece
is exposed.

My hand and part of my ribcage
rest beside my head. My feet
have been saved for special occasions. The individual strips
of flesh surround me like strains of green mold.

Yesterday was a foggy glass revealing
the skeletons that stretch between us, where our pieces
used to go. I am color-coding the days as each conversation

fades away, the words that always ended with a squeak.
One hard, yellow knob of a kneecap exposed.
These kneecaps will both be red for Tuesday.

The subtle constant helplessness
the tiny things, the big things, all the wanting
I have painted emerald green. There will be enough left over
to make into a dress, something for those that come later
to find in my refrigerator, where the milk
used to be. All the rest
has to go.

The Cavemen

I spent nearly a whole summer staring through the slats of the fence
at the people next door. We weren't allowed to talk to them
because something was wrong with them, they didn't have electricity,
they had an outhouse in the back, a pond in their yard.
Once a week, an old woman would come out of the house carrying a stack of rugs
and beat them until they were clean. I didn't understand what she was doing
thought she did it because she was angry,
like when my mom broke glasses and pop bottles in the driveway
when she was mad.

They had kids, but they were too old for us to play with
one boy had a motorcycle, like my dad, but my dad
didn't ever talk to the boy about his motorcycle. "They don't have a television!"
my mom would wonder, in those days before she got so angry
she smashed up our own set, threw a boot through the screen
ended Saturday cartoons in our house for good.

I used to wonder what it was like in their house, if they had furniture
or if they slept in piles of blankets spread over the freshly-beaten rugs
drew hieroglyphs on the walls with fingers dipped in home-made paint
huddled around a roaring fire in the middle of their living room, the smoke
disappearing through rotted slats in the ceiling.

The Dove

The bird hides inside, tucked inside my ribcage
the feathers hide my heart. You can smell its desperation on me
even through the cigarette smoke and birthday cologne
huddles dark and black and wet.

The bird is in here, barely visible
damp, white feathers pressed into a tight, red space
flailing in the sick hot summer
midnight heat. We have all become
other women over time, there is no need
to confess.

Remolding

You say I am just like that burn victim
at the hospital you volunteer at, wrapped in white sheets
and you, and only you, are responsible for my remolding
these false images in my head. These people I want to be
are just figments of my imagination, the dreams
of an enchanting nutcase
high on hygienic solvents and dreams of black-caped villains.

Your fingernails drag through my damaged skin
slough flesh off in numb, paper streamers
that hang from me like tattered moth wings. I have tried to exit
stage right so many times I've lost count. I tell
you I can dance on my own, I don't need anybody, anything
to prop me up, that I could even fly
if I just wanted it enough. You tell me

we will always be together
and that this is Paradise, right here, right now.
I just don't know it yet.

Barricade

I pretend my house is an island, Louisiana before the white men came
surrounded by the emptiness of the ocean and virginal
in the ways of vapid conversation. The wind blows in the sound of trains rumbling by
sounds like voices coming through a baby monitor, strange hands
poised to smash through glass.

I am San Juan before the Spanish landed, far from
the boy next door and the thud of the dishwasher upstairs. I can almost see
all the way to Catalina Island through the glare of streetlights
the flocks of white-winged moths and storm clouds
heavy with portent. The ripple of galleon sails

distorts the horizon, damns me to admit
white men once continued long enough down the Mississippi to find my house
did not turn around at the entrance of the Gulf of Mexico, were not dissuaded
by the piles of beer cans in my trash, the oil derricks tilted off-center in the bay
the lawn paved over to make a cracked basketball court.

Down to the Water

I close my eyes and turn left. I feel the sand beneath my bare feet
the splash of imaginary fish beneath the drunk, full moon
the thin screech of seagulls in the wind. I open my eyes and find
I am still in my back yard, a thousand miles from any beach,
an October lawn crunching beneath my feet
thin, yellow blades of grass stiff with frost.

This is not my home. I can almost smell the sweet salt ocean air
promises of warmer weather in the sanctuary of the car.
Winding cliff roads along rocky beaches call me, half a continent away
just past miles of pro-life billboards splashed with pictures of babies
cryptic, threatening Bible verses that may or may not have anything to do with
the particular stretch of highway they loom over
past miles of barbed wire separating me from herds of cows
flocks of displaced ostriches.

A Test of Vows and Faith

If a voice told you in the middle of the night
to offer the life of your child, would you
gently wake your sleeping child, tell him or her
"Get dressed, you're going to meet God."?

Would you put our daughter in the back of the car, her eyes
still blurry from sleep, tell her to put her seat belt on
as you quietly pull out of the drive
and turn the car towards the mountains? Would you

think of waking me before you left
tell me this new story about God's will
or would you hold your breath and carry your shoes
as you sneak out the door, a finger on your lips
in case our son tries to call out?

Or would you defy the command, close your ears
to the voice that promises miracles if you comply
or pile guilt on you for past gifts and love
and until you half-relent, immediately
regretting and retracting the promise of sacrifice?

The Old Green One

I will make you a music box from a porn star
fill her insides with gears and whistles, a key
that comes out of her navel for turning
in the hot summer sun
or under the stars at night.

When our daughter is older, I will explain the porn star
in the basement, tucked away with your dirty magazines
your crumpled, dented trombone. I will tell her how even music
can be base and indecent, and all that I know
about lonely breasts and constellations.

Two Minutes Thirteen Seconds

Years later, when all was forgiven, Jacob
would have Esau over to dinner
to share some of the good fortune that continued to come his way
long after none would have expected.
They would sit around their father's blessing and reminisce
about the good old days, before this thing had come between them
this glistening, sparkling promise of security
that could only be given once, to one person, at one specific time.

Sometimes, when he thought Jacob wasn't looking, Esau would try to touch the blessing
would throw pillowcases and handkerchiefs over it in an attempt
to steal it for himself. When this didn't work, he'd find the solace he sought
in his brother's wife, late at night. She never minded his rough, hairy hands
the thick pelt of fur on his neck and face, the odor of goat that clung to his body.
The weight of debt that hung between the two of them
was enough to pacify all of the regret.

The First of Many

The tiny eggs open and larvae unfurl
cluster at the edges of the birdbath as though
already dreaming of breaking free.

I try to explain to the assembled that I, too
am like one of those little black squiggles
a midge waiting to pupate and molt

spread wings and fly away, and that they are to ignore
the crumpled husk I leave behind.

I've Taken to Writing Suicide Notes

I've taken to sleeping naked at night
dreaming terrible lies beneath these stained sheets--
we meant something, we mean something, you were
just passing through.
There are places in me you can never see.

I'm practicing my handwriting, where the trembling comes in
sprawled out on the floor for invisible cameramen
to trace me in chalk, walk away.
I'm losing my mind with you inside me
you can never go,
memories, no.

The Middle of the Night

There was an explosion and I came outside. I thought I was awake
but because you were already on the porch, I must have been asleep. We must be dead.
We must have died in the explosion, everyone we know must have died
in the explosion, this is it, you said, and it was the metal voice of the vacuum cleaner
I embrace this end, infinity, us forever standing together
on the porch, waiting for the inevitable mushroom cloud
that comes with these types of explosions. I take your hand and
you pull away, a little angry, you don't want to wait out

infinity with me. There is no mushroom cloud and I realize
there must have been some sort of accident, there are bodies everywhere,
no, there are just two. Some idiot had driven right through the stop sign on our block
and had crashed into the front of someone's house. It was our house.
There are two bodies on the lawn. You are already on the porch, wide awake,
shouting to me to call the police. I must have stood there forever
with you telling me to call the police. I wanted to see the bodies up close,
to see if they were someone we knew, you said I shouldn't touch them,
I'm not supposed to move someone so soon after an accident. I nod because
that's what they say on TV, too.

Blue Car

The car appeared outside the house, as if by magic
Dropped from the sky into a pile of snow, tire tracks obliterated by fresh snow.
A sleeping bag blocked the back window completely, candy wrappers
Could be seen on the front seat.

After a couple of days, my neighbor came over and asked me if it was my car
If I wouldn't mind moving it so that her nephew could park there. I told her
How the car had just appeared in that spot, and that I didn't think anyone
Had come back for it since its arrival, although
I thought I saw a couple of people sitting in the front seat very late the night before
Hands frantically moving in the dim overhead light
But it may have been a dream.

A week or so later, a tow truck came and got the car, probably called by my neighbor
The one who came over or perhaps a different one entirely
The spot where the car had been parked was black and green with oil and antifreeze
Dirty snow and a couple of smashed beer cans. I watched the car get pulled
Backwards down the street, waited for a door to fling open angrily
In the car or in a neighboring house, but no one came out after the car
No one chased the tow truck frantically down the street.

Nebraska

just enough of a whisper of wind
to make the grass glow like the Pacific
did so long ago, the icy Pacific
calls me, half a continent away.
This is not my home.

two little girls playing in the bluffs, chasing
sandhill cranes
arms and long blond hair flapping like wings—my daughters
will never build sandcastles on crowded beaches
never play high-and-seek in abandoned lifeguard towers
never hunt imaginary fish on full moon drunk nights
or skinny-dip in frigid low-ebb tides.

I dreamed you were lying to me
and that there was way to get to the beach
if you just turned down this special street
and turned left. I felt the sand beneath my bare feet
smelled the sweet salt ocean air
and I hated you for making me feel so marooned.
This will never be my home.

A New Vocabulary

i cannot reach you
through these words:
love
don't leave me
happy birthday. so i try
on new colors: get out of here.
don't touch me.
i'm calling the police.

it's quite amazing how these shells we posses
still reach for each other, late at night
silent for moans and shuffled voices from waking dreams
shadowed and incognito. i can say your name
without screaming
here.

you humble me to infant
size, intellectually mocking
my short way of speech, my
confusion with your language
my struggle for clarity.
the key is in the ignition.
there is a full tank of gas.
i won't be home tonight. if you
hit me again, i will tell. is this
clear enough for you?

Some Babies Just Know

that they're born on thin ice
these
well-behaved children
of rape and
desertion

some babies just know
that they're born on thin ice
born prettier than the rest
born smarter
than the rest

some babies just
know
that they're born on thin ice
that the first time they screw up
they're out of a home
that they're always a hair's breadth
from a state orphanage
or a paper bag dumped
by the side of the road

some babies
just know

Spoilsport

avoiding the stares of the other visitors, he pushes his way down the aisle
to her room and close to the edge
of the hospital bed. last week, the beautiful woman was
hurtling through the air on the back of a horse
and now she would never walk again.

her breathing is so quiet he can barely hear it over the sound
of the equipment in the hospital room. a noisy machine breathes for her
but underneath it all is her own breath, soft,
a rattle of lungs inflating, deflating
a tiny whisper of life. he is here

because he knows from his own experience
her friends will all eventually abandon her, humbled
at the loss of her mobility, frightened
by her sudden dependence on them. he is here
to let her know

that no matter how beautiful she is, how beautiful she still is
she will always be alone.

Fingers Pull a Shoulder Strap Down

My ex-husband hands our son his car keys
to play with, tells him the roads are icy outside,
dangerous, that it'll be dangerous for him to drive home.
He doesn't look at me while he says this, eyes
on the child shaking the keyring noisily
standing only in a diaper. "I could die,"

he says in his best
I'm-talking-to-a-baby voice
"I could drive straight into a tree or a telephone pole
hit another car and die."
"Silly daddy," says our toddler, delighted
with the keys. He shakes them so gently
they sound like music, the different shapes and sizes
each seem to have their own sound. Underneath it all,

my ex continues to drone on about insurance policies,
my tiny apartment, how things could be
so much better for us
if he just died. So this, this moment, this
is what finally comes of best friends
clothes torn off and tossed in the corner
arms and legs entwined as though magnetized
full of dreams so real
it couldn't have happened any other way
this is how it all ends.

Overnight

He left the door open, but when the wind
blew it shut, it was locked. I knew
I should have gotten out of bed earlier
but now I'm trapped.
First I ran out of cereal, and milk
then the electricity went out so I
had to eat all the sandwich meat
before it went bad. The cheese
was warm and sweaty in the heat
but after a week in the sauna of his
apartment, I was happy to have it. Soon
the water stopped running, and I had to salvage
water from the toilet tank
and use his closets for my bathroom.
I know he's coming back
because he left all his books behind.
I know he's coming back because
he left me all these
shoes.

The Nest

I pull the bird's nest from its cradle of branches, turn it over in my hands.
Some studious bird has woven bright strips of plastic in with the straw
pasted a round piece of newspaper in at the bottom. There are birds that use
spiderwebs as glue, weave their nests entirely out of feathers and grass
others that seek out bits of aluminum foil for decoration.

I carefully put the little nest in the lilac bush, hope that someone will use it
this season as well. I don't know what a well-made nest looks like
from a bird's point of view, don't know if this one is any more spectacular
than another. It's amazing that those tiny feet and beaks can pull bits of grass and string
together to make something like this, strong enough to raise a clutch in
strong enough to last a winter in my back yard.

The Funeral

There used to be a room in the British Museum filled
with the skins of tattooed Polynesians, most of which
had died of European diseases while being paraded around the continent
and instead of returning the bodies to their homeland, or just buried
a man removed their skins, tanned them carefully, then stretched them for display
like they were animals, or some exotic tapestry imported
from a far-away kingdom.

When it was no longer fashionable to have human skins displayed on a museum's
  walls
another man came and took the skins down, rolled them up carefully like
delicate Persian rugs, stacked them in the basement. Unfortunately
the man from the first stanza didn't do a very good job of preserving the skins
perhaps because his expertise was in tanning
more durable hides, such as pigskin or calf leather,
so when a representative from the Royal Family of Hawaii came to claim the skins
to bring them home, the brittle skins were too far gone for proper identification,
gnawed on by rats and fit only for cremation.

Sparrow Poem #1

Sparrows make me think of Chairman Mao, how something so tiny
can bring a country down simply by its absence. I treasure the sparrows in my yard
all year, since they're the only birds that don't leave me when winter comes.

I wonder if they know the reason I tolerate them chasing away the other finches
goldfinches and weavers, the tiny speckled wrens
is because I admire their place in history, or because of their year-round fealty
or if they even think of me at all. My spring and summer is spent

watching the little birds mate in chirps and flutters in the tree branches
and lay claim to the birdhouses hanging from my trees. I cluck at them
from the kitchen window, refill the feeders when they're empty, I think
of all of the things Mao missed in his condemnation of sparrows
of what it must have been like that first summer without them.

The Lover of Zeus

She woke up on the beach, covered in sand
the broken arm of a starfish clutched in her fist
as if in payment for an especially horrific deed.
She dropped the single, spiky limb as soon as she knew
what it was, watched it twist in the wake before rolling
back out to sea, perhaps to grow a whole new body
perhaps in search of its old one.

There are risks that come with having trysts with a god
both to the mother and the child. She knew this,
that she might be pregnant with a bear or a wolf
or a sad, lonely thing with snakes for hair, a child
predestined to die some horrible death:
ripped apart by Amazons, gored by a bull,
nailed to a cross.

Thursday, A Little Before the School Bus is Due

How do I write about how I got from washing dishes in the kitchen
watching sparrows fighting and mating and nesting through the window over the sink
hands damp with soap bubbles and bits of last-night's dinner to here,
curled up in the yard, knees against my chest, sharp blades of dry grass
poking my cheek? There must have been a moment when I

put down the dishes and opened the door, walked down the stairs and consciously
decided to lie down on the grass, assumed this position, it all seems so important
not that I know how I got here, but that I don't move from this spot.

Some time this summer, I will build a bat house with my daughter to hang
in the tree, just above where the sparrows have all built their nests. I can see my hands
working with wood, expertly, without splinters or pain or mistakes.
Somehow, I'll get near the top of the tree, find only steady branches to balance on
nail them into place. My daughter will be so amazed, I can picture her amazement
at my carpentry skills, my tree-climbing skills, my gentle rapport with nature.
I am the best mom ever.

I close my eyes and see all of these actions so clearly I'm sure
they must already be done, there is no need to build bat houses
or paint extra bird houses, or nail anything to anything. If I can get
from the kitchen to the back yard without remembering even taking a step
then these things I can imagine in such detail, with such clarity
must already have happened without me, too.

Kiss It All Away

I crumble under the weight of your wings
as you leap from the balcony and find that you're only human
and the two of us fall.

There are gods burning in the fire place
painfully smiling through bruised lips
I've got runs in my hose from their fingernails; they need us, too.

what a disappointment it was to discover
that you still have one foot stuck in the real world
and it's the foot that counts.

For My Grandfather

Someday, your children will ask you about the war
with heavy eyes, resolve in their voices, as if
they somehow found the notes you know you burned
before they were born, as if they found
the scrap of blue fabric you still keep under the bed
ripped from the hem of a dead woman's dress.

You are older now than you were then. Once,
a woman traced the long white scars you wear across your back,
and you told her, and only her,
about that day the sun came up and everyone was dead.
That was the only time you ever spoke of the boy on the hill
his arms around his mother's waist, clinging to her dress.
You didn't know he was there until it was too late.

All the old ghosts
will be replaced by new ones, ghosts
that force your hands to do ignoble things.
You have buried the past so deep
it can never be spoken of again.

The Offering

The little bird carries the piece of fruit
from the birch tree to its nest
wriggles its brightly-colored feathers at me
song filling its throat. I carefully cut
another piece of peach, put it on the plate on the deck, wait for its return.

Later, I find that chipmunks have raided
the compost bin, left peach pits
all over the yard. I worry endlessly
about arsenic poisoning, call my husband out to help gather
the little broken bits of rough pit
search helplessly for the deadly hearts

that must be scattered everywhere.
Above, in the trees, the sparrows congregate for the evening
watch me curiously, very much
still alive.

Upon the Discovery of the Existence of Another Golden Calf

This is how God must have felt
looking down at His people dancing around the golden calf
when they thought His back was turned, surreptitiously kissing
fist-sized idols shoved deep in their pockets
when they thought He wasn't looking
whispering heresy in one another's ears
lies about other true gods that were nicer and better than Him
when they thought He couldn't hear.

Myself, I am a maelstrom of anger and defeat
hands full of hotel receipts gathered from pockets
detailing lunch dates spent beneath cheap sheets
a second cell phone full of phone numbers I don't recognize
matchbooks from nightclubs I've only seen advertised on TV.
I long to storm and gnash and wreak tidal vengeance
on all of these things that have separated him from me
blind him into submission, into acceptance, but I
know that this is not the way to bring someone back to Love.
This hopelessness, this defeat, this slow burning of love letters
from a stranger somehow better than me.

Ghost Father Father

Late at night, I swear I can still feel the impact
of his papacy, looming in the corner of the house,
an altar intact but bloody. Low, quiet, tongue lolling

in displeasure, I met my end at the dinner table every night. Anger doled out
with blessings over bread, as I wriggled in penance
and dreamed of impaled corpses. My childhood

was a warning to others that even the shadow of a thief's knowledge
could turn a child into a whore, a lunatic, and even so
I was there beside him when his breath cooled

that last, at last, an only slightly
source of subversion.

Hillsboro Bay

The jellyfish flutter just below the surface of the water, clustered together so tightly
you could walk across them to the other side. You couldn't really, of course,
you would sink right through them and end up underneath the seething cloud
of undulating tentacles, but it looks like you could just run over the top of them
if you were fast enough and light enough.

If you took a deep breath and lay flat on the swarm, on your back
arms stretched out on either side, you would probably float, and if you were lucky
the jellyfish would be clustered so tightly that the tentacles
wouldn't touch you, and then, if you turned your head slightly
so that your ear was submerged, you could hear them sing. It's like the buzzing of bees
or the thrumming of a hummingbird's wings or a chorus of angry helicopters.
Underwater, it's much louder than even standing here on the shore, watching them pass.

If you were to plunge your hands into the cloud of jellyfish just right
you could wear two of them just like a pair of gloves, and you wouldn't get stung.
You could do that with your feet, too, wear two jellyfish just like boots
and walk among them without worrying about being stung. The jellyfish you're wearing
will tell the other jellyfish that you're one of them. After a while, they'll let you swim
in their cluster, let you continue to follow them out to sea under their protection.

When Summer Comes

I bury their heads in peat and think of the day
when the sun warms the soil and the clouds bring the rain
and the white snowy fields that once seemed to stretch endless will
be a fuzzy memory of a cold and irrelevant past.
The seeds so carefully planted before the first frost
will unfold like origami and send thin furry roots tunneling
through the chilly dirt to find footholds in the earth.
I'll wake to find a thin coat of green covering
the warmed soil surrounding the base of the old birch tree
in the back yard.

Eventually, the thin frost of green will grow into a thick carpet, obscuring
the domed hills marking the entrance and exit of traveling worms,
the triangular footprints of excavating seasonal birds,
even the occasional fox footpad, preserved in wet mud. But
today, snow falls in soft clumps outside my kitchen window, barely
heard or felt by the tiny cocooned bodies of insects and plants
lying dormant beneath the soil. I stare past the snow
dream bright, grand dreams of far-off
summer days, imagining the crackle
of night crawlers moving beneath decomposing leaves, the way
the stars look so fuzzy in the sky
on hazy, summer nights.

Extractions

I did not cause this and I cannot heal this. If our love was a church,
it would be a tangle of massive roots writhing
every day, and not just today. Fingers dig deep, and even
though I sometimes I think I'm lost without your sickness
there are fingernails digging into my fists clenched tight. I compensate
by digging into the soil, wiggling around in the dirt and
willing my heart into becoming the slowest of the slow.

I have tried so hard to smooth over rough edges
struggled to placate the massive roots writhing, thick as snakes,
step aside to make way for other symptoms of destruction
phobias fluttering beneath the surface: once, you could look into my eyes,
and I into yours. But you, always, always had it worse. You
are a hard rule to set my own life against, even in times of brevity and bliss.
Out there, in the soil, the roots are coming to smooth over our rough edges.
Even sidewalks buckle under the onslaught of rippling phalanges.

Winter

These are the walls that keep us in: birds armed with flint
sharp claws curled, the children that will some day be
just like you, muddy footprints in the hallway. You tell yourself
you like it this way.

We huddle, arms and legs everywhere
one, children in the middle, something else
drops from the sky, dead, everything becomes rocks
fatal spear points for tracking down and killing monsters
chinking walls to keep us in.

Outside, the snow piles up, makes us safe.
The winter drags and we like it that way.
Buried deep inside your head is a feral creature
that can coax fire from flint, guard its territory
in ways never dreamed of by a small, brown ancestor.

Morning at the Beach

His tiny hands dig in the sand and I wince
as his fingers unearth everything from concreted cat shit to
thin bones with greasy feathers still attached but they're
all treasures to him, he shows them all to me and I
nod in appreciation at every single one.

The waves come in and sweep his findings off into the ocean,
the pile of chewed-up crab claws and fish bones
the cloudy bulbs of kelp fruit and half-dissolved plastic bags.
He cries for me to run out into the waves, after the detritus
I make a big show of stepping into the cold water, pretend to look,
shake my head at his loss.

I didn't miss you at all when you left.

You are always at my window, begging passersby
to hand me love notes, an over-jealous face behind
foggy glass, the skeletons that stretch between us
like strains of green mold.

Not the tiny things, the big things, all the wanting
the subtle constant helplessness
conversations that always ended with a squeak
I am safe from all these things
behind this blue-flecked ending.

slowly

we will not get through this.
I have spent too many nights listening
to old records, trying to find
something to tie us together.
There will be no songs between us.

you have me
afraid to come home, afraid
of walking in on you, on her,
pantomiming nightmares—
I will not sleep
with her sweat on our sheets.

we will not get through this.
I have spent too many nights
drinking suicide songs in your name,
in your memory
the places I thought we'd go
together
never existed.
We will not get through this.

This House

The trees grow close to the old house, reach out with blossom-stippled limbs
as if trying to remember. There are bodies buried beneath the layers of stucco
and drywall, a skeleton built up of skeletons stolen from a forest long ago.

If you plant a tree limb in the dirt and care for it, feed it, water it
protect it from wind and errant children's toys, it will put out tiny roots
and then bigger ones, and then one day, it will become a tree.

I'd like to image that someday, when we are long gone, and this house
has been reduced to its original pine-timber frame, those rough-hewn boards
will put out tiny roots, too, find some way back into the soil.

Conversations Deferred

I tell myself that he won't be able to find me in China
and so I sign up for language classes, learn all about tea
watch goofy romantic movies about Chinese girls and ghosts
wear long skirts to hide my enormous feet. I tell myself

that things will be better when I'm in China, that somewhere
in those cloud-topped mountains I see pictured
in cheap Chinese fans and calligraphy scrolls, I will find some cave
where I can hunker down, like a monk, and no one
will know I'm there, not even him.

Lithogenous

He screams at the car again and I feel my skin growing hard, cold
my face doesn't move as I fish another beer out of the refrigerator and
bring it out to him in the yard. He takes the beer from me with a grease-covered hand
says something about how this car could last forever so long as some stupid broad
wasn't allowed to drive it. I feel my skin turning to stone
beneath my sweater, growing cold even in the hot summer sun
I tell him I'm sorry, I don't know what happened, I'm sorry.

The sun starts to set and the car still won't move, he
says he's going out, not to wait up for him, not to let anyone else
touch the fucking car. He gets in his own car and I go back
inside the house, make myself a sandwich, turn on the TV.
Later, I'll call up the bus company, ask the operator how to get to work
from where I am, maybe look up a couple of local mechanics in the phone book
I'll think about calling them, but I won't.

Afternoons with My Stepmother

She tells me the dog park is haunted, that every time
we take the dog there, he plays more with the ghosts that he does
the other dogs, that when he starts barking at trees or birds or strangers
he's warning us that we're in a bad place. She tells me
we should find another dog park, she tells me
she's heard of a nice one a little bit farther away from home
but it's close to her church and probably free from ghosts.

She tells me the parking lot at the mall has too many ghosts
for her to buy shoes there, that every time she goes shopping
she's accosted by the same group of ill-mannered ghost children
they know she can see them so they're especially drawn to her.
She wants to got to the museum sometime, look at old photographs
see if she recognizes any of those awful children from the pictures
see if she can figure out what's wrong with them so she can offer them
some sort of help or advice, like they say to do on tv.

She tells me that she thinks her house is haunted, some new ghost
probably brought in by something she picked up at a yard sale or the thrift store.
She worries that this new ghost is attached to something she herself
is particularly attached to, the nice set of earrings she got a good deal on
at the estate sale around the corner, the almost-new glass-fronted hutch
that works so perfectly with her living room set, that ornately-carved doorstop.
She wonders if it's worth the trouble to find out how the ghost got into her house
if it just means she has to get rid of something she really likes.

The Ferret

she will not
slow down for
anything less than
promise-scent of
boiled or raw
liver or heart. Feral dreams of a past in fields. The wheel squeaks as it
spins around.

she will not
let you touch
her silk white fur

black antennae whiskers. Shivers at the sight of your gun, remembers.
will not stop
for you for
less than fingers
smeared with butter
or jam promise
not to bite
hold still. Angel vanishes in a snow drift, stark against the brown
carpet.

That Day

the last tree
at the end of the world
will wear
a human face
mouth open in a frozen scream
only withered leaves
and bleached bones
will hear.

Hands Fold Like Dying Butterflies

In sleep, he screams to be put to use
I lie about what he does during the daytime: fifteen pairs of shoes in the closet
none of them fit either of us.

There are tiny phone numbers etched into the ceiling
quotes from Mussolini and Jim Jones in the sock drawer
pictures of the six million dead in a shoe box under the bed. I know who he is

I reject his past, I reject his status, I pretend
that nothing existed before we were married. I reject
the walls of hunger between us, how useless

our life together must seem to someone like him.

Lection

Beyond the curve at the edge of the world, there is a monster that knows
who you are, an awful thing with claws and teeth and too many
eyes to miss all the bad things you do. It is watching you now.
It has an eye dedicated entirely to watching you.

There is a book that your parents are writing and it's
all about you, a list of all the terrible things you've done
since you were born, a laundry list of evils. When you are old enough
they will present this book to the monster, and it will decide
if you're worthy of passing on to adulthood. Your parents
may intervene on your behalf, but they probably won't. They know
that the monster only takes bad children, and they
can always have another one, they can try
for a good, well-behaved child next time.

Just a few children, bad children, never get to grow up, disappear into the night
from their bedrooms, dragged out the window and presumably, all the way
to the very edge of the world, where the monster lives. Who knows what the monster
does with all the children it drags back to its lair? That's not really the question
here. That is the wrong question. This, *this* is what you must take back with you
today: Try to be good. Sit still and don't fidget. Pay attention when I'm talking.
Don't lie.

Early Spring Walk

The dogs pulls at her leash because she knows everything
has changed from last week to this, that even the air is different with spring
all of the old smells have disappeared into the new grass blades pushing up
through the warm soil. The dog pulls at her leash

or perhaps, I'm the one pulling at her leash, trying to rein in the burgeoning excitement
that comes with an early spring, trying to find a way to let her know
that this could all change with a sudden snowfall, an April blizzard
a storm that could go on for days and days and days. It's hard to tell a dog
to not enjoy themselves too much because they'll only get hurt in the end,

besides, they never listen.

Holly Day has worked as a freelance writer, indexer, and editor for more than 25 years. She has over 7,000 published articles, poems, and short stories, and more than a dozen published books of fiction and nonfiction. Her book titles include *Insider's Guide to the Twin Cities, Walking Twin Cities, Music Theory for Dummies* (also released in Dutch, German, Portuguese, Spanish, French, Persian, Polish, Italian, and Russian editions), *Music Composition for Dummies* (also released in German, Portuguese, and Spanish editions), *Guitar All-in-One for Dummies, Piano All-in-One for Dummies, Nordeast Minneapolis: A History, A Brief History of Stillwater, Minnesota, The Book Of,* and the poetry books *The Smell of Snow, Late-Night Reading for Hardworking Construction Men,* and *Ugly Girl*. Her writing has been nominated for a National Magazine Award, a 49th Parallel Prize, an Isaac Asimov Award, eight Pushcart awards, and three Dzanc Book's Best of the Web awards. She is the recipient of two Midwest Writer's Grants, a Plainsongs Award, the 2011 Sam Ragan Prize for Poetry, and a Dwarf Star Award from the international-juried Science Fiction Poetry Association.

www.ingramcontent.com/pod-product-compliance
Lightning Source LLC
Chambersburg PA
CBHW070551090426

42735CB00013B/3147